I WAS HERE

A travel log of everywhere I've been and where I'm going

Books with Soul

∞

Books with Soul®
Somewhere in the desert, sea and forest.
∞
Books with Soul supports copyright for all authors.
Thank you for purchasing a copyrighted edition of this book.
First Edition 2018

Copyright © 2018 Anita Kaltenbaugh
Books with Soul Press
All rights reserved.
This book, or any portion thereof, may not be reproduced in any form
without permission.
Printed in the United States of America

ISBN-13: 978-1-949325-26-3

*Travel, the one thing you buy
that makes your richer*
-unknown

Let's get rich!

This book belongs to:

_____

It is MY travel journal and travel bucket list.

I can go wherever I want to go, with whoever I want to go with, whenever I want to go.

If you are lucky enough to BUY THIS BOOK AND start recording your vacations when you are young, hats off to you.
Imagine 20 years from now, the list of places you will be able to say:
I WAS HERE

MAKE IT A HABIT. RECORD EACH VACATION IN THE BACK OF THIS BOOK WHEN YOU UNPACK.

Remember, this is your life,
See what you want to
See.
Go where you want to go.
Make a plan,
And it will
Happen.

Scribble, write, erase, draw,
doodle, or tell a story.
Write important dates down, journal,
write a song, write a poem, write words.
Keep a record of every adventure in your
lifetime.
This is your space.
Someday you'll be glad you kept this notebook
and you'll treasure your dreams.

Introduction

This book is for YOUR journey.

The places you will explore in your lifetime.

Where do you want to go? What do you want to see?

The world is yours to traverse, and there are so many choices of places to stop and get off.
So, let me be the first to congratulate you.

Congratulations.
You are way ahead of most of the world. You are creating a Travel Record of every place on earth you will step foot on. Dreaming on paper, making the words a possible reality. Writing things down with pen or pencil. Writing things down is the first step to making them become reality. There is something empowering about looking at the words that were in your head, now on paper

"If you don't know where you are going, how will you know when you get there?" It's true, we often need a road map of where we are headed, and yet sometimes, it's the journey getting to our designated point that ends up changing our lives.

It doesn't matter if you begin your travels when you are 15, 21, 35, 43, 50, 66, 75 or 90 years old. It only matters that you began.

Where do you want to go? What do you want to see?

Do you want to travel to every continent on earth?
Do you want to see every state in your country?

Some folks desire to see every state in
the United States, or every country in Europe,
South America, Africa, or Asia. Some might have a list of local places they have never taken the time or energy to see.

There are no wrong answers.

It is about what you want.

My travel bucket list consists of a stop at every continent.

How many continents are there? Well, depending on geologists and scientist research, you might find conflicting answers. Some experts state 6 continents (Europe and Asia or Eurasia as 1), some state 7 and break them out, and recently there is discussion about a new continent, Zealandia (New Zealand and New Caledonia) so that would make 7 or 8. Confusing? Yes, I know. But, who cares? This is not that kind of book.

In this book, there are no rules. You can create your travel bucket list, add to it, or delete from it. You are in charge and you can change it as many times as you like.

For the purpose of this book let's go with the 7 continents of the world as: North America, South America, Antarctica, Europe, Asia, Africa and Australia. And as of right now, I have three continents to go to fulfill my goal.

I've been fortunate to travel often and a few years ago I logged over 99 vacations in three years. I even wrote a book about how I was able to plan and afford my journey. *Travel Secrets: An Insider guide to planning, affording and taking more vacations.*

So, where do you want to go?

This is a journal to figure out what destinations *you* most desire to explore. Where does your heart or your mind escape to when you have that moment of peace? What have you been longing to see up close? Maybe it's around the corner, or far away. There are no right answers.
It's a big world out there and the list of possibilities of places to explore are endless.

This is a book to keep a log of all your travels.

Write down every vacation you take in a year,
a decade, and in your life.
Share them with your
family or friends.

Leave this journal for your parents, children,
best friend or closest companions.

Or, perhaps just keep it for yourself, with a cord tied around it and see how many places on the amp you can   go and how many bucket items you can achieve.

Check the boxes.
Cross out the names and places you visited, write the date you traveled beside the names on your list.

Write in this book, draw in it, doodle, scribble, do what you wish.

Paste photos of places you long to go. Pictures you ripped out of a magazine. Carry it in the rain, bend the pages, rip a few out—just do what you want.

It doesn't matter, there are no rules. It is your Travel Journal.

Do with it whatever you choose to do.

Whatever you do, create your Travel Bucket List, and take more vacations.

We live in a remarkable era of technology –
   and because of this, travel has never been easier, more accessible or more affordable.

We only have ourselves to blame for not planning more time off to visit the destinations that are alive in our mind.

I WAS HERE

Take the time in your life to figure out your
Travel Bucket List,
and then get busy making it happen.

If you dream it, it can happen.

EXPLORE and take notes, so you can have a written history of your adventures.

The first step of a living your travel dreams,
is knowing where and what they are.
Create a road map and set goals.

If you want to travel more figure out where?

And please...when you return from every vacation, write
in the back of this book:
where you visited,
where you stayed,
who you went with and one favorite moment.

You'll think you will always remember, but if you are fortunate to live a long life, and travel, someday you will be so thankful you recorded the moments.

Imagine 10 years from now...you will have collected memories of all the vacations, adventures and voyages in the back of this book.

*See the world,
by writing it down,
you are on the road to achieving it.*

"The world is a book and those who do not travel read only one page."

– *St. Augustine*

I WAS HERE

Okay, try to complete a beginning list of where you want to go. You are brainstorming. You will have room at the back of the book, to make a final list.

I WAS HERE

LET'S THINK ABOUT

MY TOP 5 PLACES TO SEE

THE FIRST 5 LOCATIONS THAT POP IN MY MIND
THEY CAN BE ANYWHERE ON THIS PLANET

I WAS HERE

LET'S THINK ABOUT
PLACES I DREAM OF
THE FIRST TEN PLACES THAT POP IN MY MIND

List of the 7 continents:

North America:

South America:

Europe:

Asia:

Australia:

Antartica:

Africa:

I WAS HERE

LET'S THINK ABOUT :

PLACES I WANT TO SEE IN THE USA

LET'S THINK ABOUT :

PLACES I WANT TO SEE IN CENTRAL AMERICA

I WAS HERE

LET'S THINK ABOUT :

PLACES I WANT TO SEE IN EUROPE

LET'S THINK ABOUT :

PLACES I WANT TO SEE IN AUSTRALIA./NEW ZEALAND/NEW CALEDONIA

I WAS HERE

LET'S THINK ABOUT :

PLACES I WANT TO SEE IN ASIA

LET'S THINK ABOUT :

PLACES I WANT TO SEE IN A DAY'S DRIVE

I WAS HERE

LET'S THINK ABOUT :

PLACES I WANT TO SEE IN MY 50 MILE RADIUS

LET'S THINK ABOUT
FAVORITE VACATIONS
WHY DID I LOVE THEM?

Use this list,

"MY Travel Bucket List" as a place to start. Change it as many times as you want. Go through the rest of the journal. Write your thoughts, ideas, scribble, doodle, and answer a few of the questions, or read the quotes. Imagine the places, dream destinations, and off the beaten hidden gems you have longed to visit. Research exciting images online. Make a list of new locations. Brainstorm.

At the back of the book is another blank travel bucket list. You can write your new travel bucket list there, after you have worked your way through the pages.

"To live is the rarest thing in the world. Most people exist, that is all." Oscar Wilde

I WAS HERE

MY TRAVEL BUCKET LIST

DATE :
TOP 10 PLACES I WANT TO SEE

So where do you want to go next?

"Life is either a daring adventure or nothing."

-- Helen Keller

Plan. Otherwise it's all talk.

I WAS HERE

Tired of hotel rooms? Want a home away from home?
Try Airbnb.
Airbnb is my favorite way to travel. It's so much more than just a bed and bathroom.
Experience how it feels to live like a local. I have stayed in an oceanfront condo in the Dominican Republic, a beach house in Santa Cruz, CA, a loft in Knoxville, TN and many more. Every rental has been awesome.

If you have never used Airbnb, use this code on a first-time reservation and receive $40 off.

(Airbnb can change this offer at any time and is only for first time users of Airbnb.)

For $40 off first reservation. Paste this link or click on this link and sign up:
www.airbnb.com/c/anitak103

Live in the sunshine, swim in the sea, drink the wild air- Ralph Waldo Emerson

I WAS HERE

I see a photo of this destination and I can't stop thinking about it:

I haven't been everywhere, but it sounds like a great place.

I WAS HERE

Remember when you travel, pause, and live in the moment of where you are.

Where?

I WAS HERE

Life is too short, make your list, and get busy living.

Sometimes, I want to escape all the stress and go here:

I WAS HERE

Take the Travel Quiz and discover what kind of traveler you are:

Do you think you like variety or the same type of vacations? Answer the questions and score. This exercise will help you start to make a bucket list you will enjoy.

I WAS HERE

Quiz: What kind of traveler are you?
Take the following quiz. Read the questions out loud and answer the questions as an individual. Score to find out what kind of traveler you are. Compare answers as a couple.

1. In my mind, the word vacation conjures up an image that fits in one of these categories:
   a. Beach scene, island, tropical
   b. Skyscrapers, vibrant city scene, fantastic food
   c. Woods, forest, trails, trees
   d. Landmarks, old castles, museums, history
2. If I had to choose one of the following activities to do on my vacation, I would choose:
   a. A lounge chair, blue water, a good book, a frozen cocktail
   b. Sightseeing, trains, night clubs, shopping
   c. Hiking, skiing, camping, biking
   d. Tours to little known places, art, history, knowledge
3. You scored a free vacation, which one would you pick?
   a. All-inclusive resort vacation in Turks and Caicos
   b. 4 nights in Manhattan, with show tickets
   c. An RV for a week in Colorado
   d. A European guided tour of castles.
4. Which type of movie/series do you most want to watch?
   a. Bay Watch, Fools Gold, Secret islands of the world. or Cocktail
   b. Sex and the City, Man on the Ledge, Foodie City Style
   c. Into the Wild, The Edge, The Great Outdoors, Everest
   d. Downton Abbey, The Da Vinci Code, The History channel
5. Pick a song out of the following you would like to hear right now:
   a. No Shoes No Shirt No problem
   b. New York New York
   c. Take me Home Country Road
   d. Brahms Symphony No 1

6. What do you most feel like packing on a trip?
    a. Bathing suits, shorts, t-shirts, flip flops, beachy dresses
    b. Fly clothes, club clothes, clothes that make a statement
    c. hiking boots, shorts, hats, jeans, outdoor wear
    d. Comfortable clothes, walking shoes, things that pack well
7. Pick a food that sounds good to you in this moment:
    a. Shrimp, fish, fresh fruit, tropical salads, lobster
    b. Tapas, foie gras, steak, eclectic dishes, sashimi
    c. Hamburgers, hotdogs, grilled steaks, barbeque
    d. Local dishes, chocolate, Indian food, German schnitzel
8. Pick a drink you would like to order:
    a. Margarita, frozen cocktail, island local beer
    b. Cosmopolitan, champagne, Harvey wall banger,
    c. Beer, vodka, wine
    d. Pilsner, tea, coffee, port
9. Would you rather?
    a. Sit on a lounge chair listening to the waves
    b. Read your newspaper in the middle of a city outdoor café
    c. Stretch out on a blanket in the middle of the woods
    d. Eat lunch at a café in the middle of an Art Museum

Count 1 for every a, b, c, d, you have:

A= _____

B= _____

C= _____

D= _____

I WAS HERE

Answers:

A- If you have 6-9 A's, Hello beach lover. Islands, tropical weather & toes in the sand sounds like a great vacation to you. Pick an island you have never stepped foot on and go!

B- If you have 6-9 B's, you thrive in the city. People watching, night life and the energy of the crowds wake you up. Check out a city center you have never visited and immerse yourself in the city.

C- If you scored 6-9 C's, you are a back to nature kind of person. Explore the off the beaten track places. Hike to somewhere most people never see in their lifetime.

D- If you scored 6-9 D's, you love history. You seek out places that tell a story, locations that shed light on where we came from. Check out a medieval city, or a city in the national historic registry.

3-5 A's, you like the beach, it's on your list, but you like to mix it up with a variety of vacations.

3-5 B's, you enjoy the city. but you like variety & change

3-5 C's, you love nature and off the beaten track but not all the time.

3-5 D's, History is fascinating to you, and you want to explore a slice of it on your vacation.

1-2 A's, the beach is not your first choice, but you will try a tropical vacation if your other half wants to.

1-2 B's, the city is okay for some things.

1-2 C's. You can visit nature but not please no camping.

1-2 D's, you enjoy a little history, maybe 1 museum every 2 years.

Zero A's, don't go to the beach.

Zero B's, stay away from the city for vacations.

Zero C's, stay out of the woods.

Zero D's, take a nap while your partner goes to a museum.

I WAS HERE

Run away
(even if it's only for a week)

Do you know how many countries there are in the world?

I WAS HERE

There are 193 or 195 countries in the world, depending on how you look at it.

List of all the countries in the world:

A

- Afghanistan
- Albania
- Algeria
- Andorra
- Angola
- Antigua and Barbuda
- Argentina
- Armenia
- Aruba
- Australia
- Austria
- Azerbaijan

B

- Bahamas, The
- Bahrain
- Bangladesh
- Barbados
- Belarus
- Belgium
- Belize
- Benin
- Bhutan
- Bolivia
- Bosnia and Herzegovina
- Botswana
- Brazil
- Brunei
- Bulgaria
- Burkina Faso
- Burma
- Burundi

I WAS HERE

C

- Cambodia
- Cameroon
- Canada
- Cabo Verde
- Central African Republic

- Chad
- Chile
- China
- Colombia
- Comoros
- Congo, Democratic Republic of the
- Congo, Republic of the
- Costa Rica
- Cote d'Ivoire
- Croatia
- Cuba
- Curacao
- Cyprus
- Czechia

D

- Denmark
- Djibouti
- Dominica
- Dominican Republic

E

- East Timor (see Timor-Leste)
- Ecuador
- Egypt
- El Salvador

- Equatorial Guinea
- Eritrea
- Estonia
- Ethiopia

F

- Fiji
- Finland
- France

G

- Gabon
- Gambia, The
- Georgia
- Germany

- Ghana
- Greece
- Grenada
- Guatemala
- Guinea
- Guinea-Bissau
- Guyana

H

- Haiti
- Holy See
- Honduras
- Hong Kong
- Hungary

I

- Iceland
- India
- Indonesia
- Iran

I WAS HERE

- Iraq
- Ireland
- Israel
- Italy

J

- Jamaica
- Japan
- Jordan

K

- Kazakhstan
- Kenya
- Kiribati
- Korea, North
- Korea, South
- Kosovo
- Kuwait
- Kyrgyzstan

L

- Laos
- Latvia
- Lebanon
- Lesotho
- Liberia
- Libya
- Liechtenstein
- Lithuania
- Luxembourg

M

- Macau
- Macedonia
- Madagascar
- Malawi
- Malaysia

- Maldives
- Mali
- Malta
- Marshall Islands
- Mauritania
- Mauritius
- Mexico
- Micronesia
- Moldova
- Monaco
- Mongolia
- Montenegro
- Morocco
- Mozambique

N

- Namibia
- Nauru
- Nepal
- Netherlands
- New Zealand
- Nicaragua
- Niger
- Nigeria
- North Korea
- Norway

O

- Oman

P

- Pakistan
- Palau
- Palestinian Territories
- Panama
- Papua New Guinea
- Paraguay
- Peru

I WAS HERE

- Philippines
- Poland
- Portugal

Q

- Qatar

R

- Romania
- Russia
- Rwanda

S

- Saint Kitts and Nevis
- Saint Lucia
- Saint Vincent and the Grenadines
- Samoa
- San Marino
- Sao Tome and Principe
- Saudi Arabia
- Senegal
- Serbia
- Seychelles
- Sierra Leone
- Singapore
- Sint Maarten
- Slovakia
- Slovenia
- Solomon Islands
- Somalia
- South Africa
- South Korea
- South Sudan
- Spain
- Sri Lanka
- Sudan
- Suriname

- Swaziland
- Sweden
- Switzerland
- Syria

T

- Taiwan
- Tajikistan
- Tanzania
- Thailand
- Timor-Leste
- Togo
- Tonga
- Trinidad and Tobago
- Tunisia
- Turkey
- Turkmenistan
- Tuvalu

U

- Uganda
- Ukraine
- United Arab Emirates
- United Kingdom
- Uruguay
- Uzbekistan

V

- Vanuatu
- Venezuela
- Vietnam

Y

- Yemen

Z

- Zambia
- Zimbabwe

I WAS HERE

Put a checkmark by the countries you have never heard of.

Circle the countries you want to visit.

Look up the ones you need more information.

Pick one country that is the road less traveled, and have an adventure of a lifetime.

You can do this...Explore our planet.

The list of countries can differ from different sources. This list is from:

The U.S. Department of State.

https://www.state.gov/misc/list/index.htm

I WAS HERE

If I only knew that magical place--that magical spot that makes me feel at home, and yet I have never been there?

∞ infinite possibilities

I WAS HERE

Die with memories not dreams -unknown

Sometimes we just need to say "Yes" more often…

I WAS HERE

If you found a magic bottle and a travel genie popped out granting you 3 vacations, anywhere in the world? Where would you choose?

1.
2.
3.

You can never cross the ocean until you have the courage to lose sight of the shore.
Christopher Columbus

Though we travel the world over to find the beautiful, we must carry it with us, or we find it not.
Ralph Waldo Emerson

Fill your life with adventures not things. Have stories to tell not to stuff to show.

Will you follow your dreams?

Write your top 2 travel destinations on a piece
of paper.
include your email address and your name,
Write, "This is where we want to Travel to..."
Roll it up, place it in a bottle
and ... wait for it... don't toss it out to sea.
It will probably end up in a floating garbage dump.

So, instead ... hide it somewhere you might find it in the future, or where someone else might discover it.

Who knows... when you see it years later, maybe your travel dreams came true.

I WAS HERE

Travel the one thing that cost money but makes you richer. -
Unknown

The sea lives in every one of us.- *Wyland*

Make a list of places by the Sea you want to SEE:

I WAS HERE

The whole secret of a successful life is to find out what is one's destiny to do, and then do it." -- *Henry Ford*

"You only live once, but if you do it right, once is enough." -- *Mae West*

I WAS HERE

Travel far enough, and you may find out who you really are. A.K. Smith

"It does not matter how slowly you go,
so long as you do not stop."
- *Confucius*

I WAS HERE

Traveling it leaves you speechless, then turns you into a storyteller.
IBN BATTUTA

"Learn from yesterday, live for today, hope for tomorrow. The important thing is not to stop questioning."
-- *Albert Einstein*

I WAS HERE

Traveling makes one **modest,** you see the tiny space **you occupy** in the **world.** -Gustave Flaubert

Why travel?
Why breathe
or exist?

Travel outside your box.

I WAS HERE

The world is big and I want to get a good look at it before it gets dark.- John Muir

If you schedule vacations like doctor appointments, you will improve your health.

I WAS HERE

Just go.

Get away from it all or get into it all.

I dare you.

Better to see something once than hear about it a thousand times. - Asian Proverb

How do you know if you like this or that if you've never tried it?

I WAS HERE

"He who does not travel does not know the value of men."– Moorish proverb

Open your mind and see the world.

Be accepting without be judgmental and the world will be AMAZING.

This is my bucket list. I can go where I want to go, see what I want to see.

I WAS HERE

I watched a movie, and now I want to go here:

I WAS HERE

I heard about this place:

Pick a weekend once a month and get away, even if it's close by.

I WAS HERE

Plan your vacations and they will happen.

If you never plan to get away, you won't go.

I WAS HERE

If we were meant to stay in one place, we'd have roots instead of feet. - anon

. "Happiness is a butterfly, which when pursued, is always beyond your grasp, but which, if you will sit down quietly, may alight upon you." -- *Nathaniel Hawthorne*

I WAS HERE

Only put off until tomorrow what you are willing to die having left undone."
-Pablo Picasso

Bid on a travel auction. It might be the one destination you didn't even know you were supposed to visit.

(tip: try Luxury Link or Google Travel auctions)

I WAS HERE

. "You may only succeed if you desire succeeding; you may only fail if you do not mind failing." — *Philippos*

Don't fail at creating a travel bucket list and recording all your trips in this book. YOU CAN DO IT!

Have you thought of 3 new places you might want to see? Write them down.

I WAS HERE

One of the best Vacations Ever:

Go see the world the way you want.

"Twenty years from now you will be more disappointed by the things that you didn't do than by the ones you did do. So, throw off the bowlines. Sail away from the safe harbor. Catch the trade winds in your sails. Explore. Dream. Discover."
- Mark Twain

We travel not to escape life, but for life to escape us -unknown

I WAS HERE

"Keep your face to the sunshine and you can never see the shadow."

- Helen Keller

"Be yourself. Everyone else is already taken." -- *Oscar Wilde*

I WAS HERE

Pick a letter in the alphabet, any letter. Look at the list of 195 countries under that letter pick one!

It is never too late to be what you might have been. - George Eliot

I WAS HERE

Adventure is worthwhile - Aesop

If I want to go somewhere, see a specific destination…then I need to figure out a way to make it happen.

I WAS HERE

For my part, I travel not to go anywhere,
but to go, I travel for
travel's sake.
The great affair is to move.
-Robert Louis Stevenson

See the world, maybe even the moon.

I WAS HERE

We travel, some of us forever, to seek other places, other lives, other words. - Anais Nin

I dream of this place:

I WAS HERE

Life is too short not to have a little sand in your suitcase. Anita Kaltenbaugh

Go.

I WAS HERE

See.

Actually, the best gift you could have given her was a lifetime of adventures...
Lewis Carroll Alice in Wonderland

I WAS HERE

Go find your Alice

What's your favorite season?

Where can you travel and experience that season?

I WAS HERE

Go to a place with the weather you love.

They say there's a place at the end of the rainbow filled with gold…go forth and find your end of the rainbow…wherever it is, you'll find riches better than gold. A.K. Smith

I WAS HERE

Dream your destination.

Take me:

I WAS HERE

**I love the people who travel to the edge of the sea,
they are the ones who will never give up.**
A.K. Smith

If we can imagine a place of beauty and peace
than we must find it...

I WAS HERE

I want to use this mode of transportation on my next trip:

If I close my eyes I picture myself here:

I WAS HERE

Focus more on your desire than your doubt, and the dream will take care of itself.
Mark Twain

To move, to breathe, to fly, to float, to roam the roads of lands remote, to travel is to live.
Hans Christian Andersen

I WAS HERE

Always take the scenic route

I'm ready.

Just like people, the world is more amazing upfront in person, than on the internet.

Let's be in the moment! No streaming, put the phone down, look up and see the world in person.
A.K. Smith

I WAS HERE

I need to save money to go here:

When I want to be free, I go to the sea, that is where I find freedom.
A.K. Smith

I WAS HERE

And so the adventure begins

If you plan, you can go anywhere in the world.

Anywhere.

If you are lucky enough to start recording your vacations when you are young, Fantastic.
Imagine 20 years from now-- the places you will be able to say:

I WAS HERE

I WAS HERE

MY TRAVEL LOG

DATE:
STATE, COUNTRY:
WHERE I SLEPT:

WHO I WENT WITH:
FAVORITE MOMENT:

DATE:
STATE, COUNTRY:
WHERE I SLEPT:

WHO I WENT WITH:
FAVORITE MOMENT:

I WAS HERE

MY TRAVEL LOG

DATE:
STATE, COUNTRY:
WHERE I SLEPT:

WHO I WENT WITH:
FAVORITE MOMENT:

DATE:
STATE, COUNTRY:
WHERE I SLEPT:

WHO I WENT WITH:
FAVORITE MOMENT:

MY TRAVEL LOG

DATE:
STATE, COUNTRY:
WHERE I SLEPT:

WHO I WENT WITH:
FAVORITE MOMENT:

DATE:
STATE, COUNTRY:
WHERE I SLEPT:

WHO I WENT WITH:
FAVORITE MOMENT:

I WAS HERE

MY TRAVEL LOG

DATE:
STATE, COUNTRY:
WHERE I SLEPT:

WHO I WENT WITH:
FAVORITE MOMENT:

DATE:
STATE, COUNTRY:
WHERE I SLEPT:

WHO I WENT WITH:
FAVORITE MOMENT:

MY TRAVEL LOG

DATE:
STATE, COUNTRY:
WHERE I SLEPT:

WHO I WENT WITH:
FAVORITE MOMENT:

DATE:
STATE, COUNTRY:
WHERE I SLEPT:

WHO I WENT WITH:
FAVORITE MOMENT:

I WAS HERE

MY TRAVEL LOG

DATE:
STATE, COUNTRY:
WHERE I SLEPT:

WHO I WENT WITH:
FAVORITE MOMENT:

DATE:
STATE, COUNTRY:
WHERE I SLEPT:

WHO I WENT WITH:
FAVORITE MOMENT:

MY TRAVEL LOG

DATE:
STATE, COUNTRY:
WHERE I SLEPT:

WHO I WENT WITH:
FAVORITE MOMENT:

DATE:
STATE, COUNTRY:
WHERE I SLEPT:

WHO I WENT WITH:
FAVORITE MOMENT:

I WAS HERE

MY TRAVEL LOG

DATE:
STATE, COUNTRY:
WHERE I SLEPT:

WHO I WENT WITH:
FAVORITE MOMENT:

DATE:
STATE, COUNTRY:
WHERE I SLEPT:

WHO I WENT WITH:
FAVORITE MOMENT:

MY TRAVEL LOG

DATE:
STATE, COUNTRY:
WHERE I SLEPT:

WHO I WENT WITH:
FAVORITE MOMENT:

DATE:
STATE, COUNTRY:
WHERE I SLEPT:

WHO I WENT WITH:
FAVORITE MOMENT:

I WAS HERE

MY TRAVEL LOG

DATE:
STATE, COUNTRY:
WHERE I SLEPT:

WHO I WENT WITH:
FAVORITE MOMENT:

DATE:
STATE, COUNTRY:
WHERE I SLEPT:

WHO I WENT WITH:
FAVORITE MOMENT:

MY TRAVEL LOG

DATE:
STATE, COUNTRY:
WHERE I SLEPT:

WHO I WENT WITH:
FAVORITE MOMENT:

DATE:
STATE, COUNTRY:
WHERE I SLEPT:

WHO I WENT WITH:
FAVORITE MOMENT:

I WAS HERE

MY TRAVEL LOG

DATE:
STATE, COUNTRY:
WHERE I SLEPT:

WHO I WENT WITH:
FAVORITE MOMENT:

DATE:
STATE, COUNTRY:
WHERE I SLEPT:

WHO I WENT WITH:
FAVORITE MOMENT:

MY TRAVEL LOG

DATE:
STATE, COUNTRY:
WHERE I SLEPT:

WHO I WENT WITH:
FAVORITE MOMENT:

DATE:
STATE, COUNTRY:
WHERE I SLEPT:

WHO I WENT WITH:
FAVORITE MOMENT:

I WAS HERE

MY TRAVEL LOG

DATE:
STATE, COUNTRY:
WHERE I SLEPT:

WHO I WENT WITH:
FAVORITE MOMENT:

DATE:
STATE, COUNTRY:
WHERE I SLEPT:

WHO I WENT WITH:
FAVORITE MOMENT:

MY TRAVEL LOG

DATE:
STATE, COUNTRY:
WHERE I SLEPT:

WHO I WENT WITH:
FAVORITE MOMENT:

DATE:
STATE, COUNTRY:
WHERE I SLEPT:

WHO I WENT WITH:
FAVORITE MOMENT:

I WAS HERE

MY TRAVEL LOG

DATE:
STATE, COUNTRY:
WHERE I SLEPT:

WHO I WENT WITH:
FAVORITE MOMENT:

DATE:
STATE, COUNTRY:
WHERE I SLEPT:

WHO I WENT WITH:
FAVORITE MOMENT:

MY TRAVEL LOG

DATE:
STATE, COUNTRY:
WHERE I SLEPT:

WHO I WENT WITH:
FAVORITE MOMENT:

DATE:
STATE, COUNTRY:
WHERE I SLEPT:

WHO I WENT WITH:
FAVORITE MOMENT:

I WAS HERE

MY TRAVEL LOG

DATE:
STATE, COUNTRY:
WHERE I SLEPT:

WHO I WENT WITH:
FAVORITE MOMENT:

DATE:
STATE, COUNTRY:
WHERE I SLEPT:

WHO I WENT WITH:
FAVORITE MOMENT:

MY TRAVEL LOG

DATE:
STATE, COUNTRY:
WHERE I SLEPT:

WHO I WENT WITH:
FAVORITE MOMENT:

DATE:
STATE, COUNTRY:
WHERE I SLEPT:

WHO I WENT WITH:
FAVORITE MOMENT:

I WAS HERE

MY TRAVEL LOG

DATE:
STATE, COUNTRY:
WHERE I SLEPT:

WHO I WENT WITH:
FAVORITE MOMENT:

DATE:
STATE, COUNTRY:
WHERE I SLEPT:

WHO I WENT WITH:
FAVORITE MOMENT:

MY TRAVEL LOG

DATE:
STATE, COUNTRY:
WHERE I SLEPT:

WHO I WENT WITH:
FAVORITE MOMENT:

DATE:
STATE, COUNTRY:
WHERE I SLEPT:

WHO I WENT WITH:
FAVORITE MOMENT:

I WAS HERE

MY TRAVEL LOG

DATE:
STATE, COUNTRY:
WHERE I SLEPT:

WHO I WENT WITH:
FAVORITE MOMENT:

DATE:
STATE, COUNTRY:
WHERE I SLEPT:

WHO I WENT WITH:
FAVORITE MOMENT:

MY TRAVEL LOG

DATE:
STATE, COUNTRY:
WHERE I SLEPT:

WHO I WENT WITH:
FAVORITE MOMENT:

DATE:
STATE, COUNTRY:
WHERE I SLEPT:

WHO I WENT WITH:
FAVORITE MOMENT:

I WAS HERE

MY TRAVEL LOG

DATE:
STATE, COUNTRY:
WHERE I SLEPT:

WHO I WENT WITH:
FAVORITE MOMENT:

DATE:
STATE, COUNTRY:
WHERE I SLEPT:

WHO I WENT WITH:
FAVORITE MOMENT:

MY TRAVEL LOG

DATE:
STATE, COUNTRY:
WHERE I SLEPT:

WHO I WENT WITH:
FAVORITE MOMENT:

DATE:
STATE, COUNTRY:
WHERE I SLEPT:

WHO I WENT WITH:
FAVORITE MOMENT:

I WAS HERE

MY TRAVEL LOG

DATE:
STATE, COUNTRY:
WHERE I SLEPT:

WHO I WENT WITH:
FAVORITE MOMENT:

DATE:
STATE, COUNTRY:
WHERE I SLEPT:

WHO I WENT WITH:
FAVORITE MOMENT:

MY TRAVEL LOG

DATE:
STATE, COUNTRY:
WHERE I SLEPT:

WHO I WENT WITH:
FAVORITE MOMENT:

DATE:
STATE, COUNTRY:
WHERE I SLEPT:

WHO I WENT WITH:
FAVORITE MOMENT:

I WAS HERE

MY TRAVEL LOG

DATE:
STATE, COUNTRY:
WHERE I SLEPT:

WHO I WENT WITH:
FAVORITE MOMENT:

DATE:
STATE, COUNTRY:
WHERE I SLEPT:

WHO I WENT WITH:
FAVORITE MOMENT:

MY TRAVEL LOG

DATE:
STATE, COUNTRY:
WHERE I SLEPT:

WHO I WENT WITH:
FAVORITE MOMENT:

DATE:
STATE, COUNTRY:
WHERE I SLEPT:

WHO I WENT WITH:
FAVORITE MOMENT:

I WAS HERE

MY TRAVEL LOG

DATE:
STATE, COUNTRY:
WHERE I SLEPT:

WHO I WENT WITH:
FAVORITE MOMENT:

DATE:
STATE, COUNTRY:
WHERE I SLEPT:

WHO I WENT WITH:
FAVORITE MOMENT:

MY TRAVEL LOG

DATE:
STATE, COUNTRY:
WHERE I SLEPT:

WHO I WENT WITH:
FAVORITE MOMENT:

DATE:
STATE, COUNTRY:
WHERE I SLEPT:

WHO I WENT WITH:
FAVORITE MOMENT:

I WAS HERE

MY TRAVEL LOG

DATE:
STATE, COUNTRY:
WHERE I SLEPT:

WHO I WENT WITH:
FAVORITE MOMENT:

DATE:
STATE, COUNTRY:
WHERE I SLEPT:

WHO I WENT WITH:
FAVORITE MOMENT:

MY TRAVEL LOG

DATE:
STATE, COUNTRY:
WHERE I SLEPT:

WHO I WENT WITH:
FAVORITE MOMENT:

DATE:
STATE, COUNTRY:
WHERE I SLEPT:

WHO I WENT WITH:
FAVORITE MOMENT:

I WAS HERE

MY TRAVEL LOG

DATE:
STATE, COUNTRY:
WHERE I SLEPT:

WHO I WENT WITH:
FAVORITE MOMENT:

DATE:
STATE, COUNTRY:
WHERE I SLEPT:

WHO I WENT WITH:
FAVORITE MOMENT:

MY TRAVEL LOG

DATE:
STATE, COUNTRY:
WHERE I SLEPT:

WHO I WENT WITH:
FAVORITE MOMENT:

DATE:
STATE, COUNTRY:
WHERE I SLEPT:

WHO I WENT WITH:
FAVORITE MOMENT:

I WAS HERE

MY TRAVEL LOG

DATE:
STATE, COUNTRY:
WHERE I SLEPT:

WHO I WENT WITH:
FAVORITE MOMENT:

DATE:
STATE, COUNTRY:
WHERE I SLEPT:

WHO I WENT WITH:
FAVORITE MOMENT:

MY TRAVEL LOG

DATE:
STATE, COUNTRY:
WHERE I SLEPT:

WHO I WENT WITH:
FAVORITE MOMENT:

DATE:
STATE, COUNTRY:
WHERE I SLEPT:

WHO I WENT WITH:
FAVORITE MOMENT:

I WAS HERE

MY TRAVEL LOG

DATE:
STATE, COUNTRY:
WHERE I SLEPT:

WHO I WENT WITH:
FAVORITE MOMENT:

DATE:
STATE, COUNTRY:
WHERE I SLEPT:

WHO I WENT WITH:
FAVORITE MOMENT:

MY TRAVEL LOG

DATE:
STATE, COUNTRY:
WHERE I SLEPT:

WHO I WENT WITH:
FAVORITE MOMENT:

DATE:
STATE, COUNTRY:
WHERE I SLEPT:

WHO I WENT WITH:
FAVORITE MOMENT:

I WAS HERE

MY TRAVEL LOG

DATE:
STATE, COUNTRY:
WHERE I SLEPT:

WHO I WENT WITH:
FAVORITE MOMENT:

DATE:
STATE, COUNTRY:
WHERE I SLEPT:

WHO I WENT WITH:
FAVORITE MOMENT:

MY TRAVEL LOG

DATE:
STATE, COUNTRY:
WHERE I SLEPT:

WHO I WENT WITH:
FAVORITE MOMENT:

DATE:
STATE, COUNTRY:
WHERE I SLEPT:

WHO I WENT WITH:
FAVORITE MOMENT:

I WAS HERE

MY TRAVEL LOG

DATE:
STATE, COUNTRY:
WHERE I SLEPT:

WHO I WENT WITH:
FAVORITE MOMENT:

DATE:
STATE, COUNTRY:
WHERE I SLEPT:

WHO I WENT WITH:
FAVORITE MOMENT:

MY TRAVEL LOG

DATE:
STATE, COUNTRY:
WHERE I SLEPT:

WHO I WENT WITH:
FAVORITE MOMENT:

DATE:
STATE, COUNTRY:
WHERE I SLEPT:

WHO I WENT WITH:
FAVORITE MOMENT:

I WAS HERE

MY TRAVEL LOG

DATE:
STATE, COUNTRY:
WHERE I SLEPT:

WHO I WENT WITH:
FAVORITE MOMENT:

DATE:
STATE, COUNTRY:
WHERE I SLEPT:

WHO I WENT WITH:
FAVORITE MOMENT:

MY TRAVEL LOG

DATE:
STATE, COUNTRY:
WHERE I SLEPT:

WHO I WENT WITH:
FAVORITE MOMENT:

DATE:
STATE, COUNTRY:
WHERE I SLEPT:

WHO I WENT WITH:
FAVORITE MOMENT:

I WAS HERE

MY TRAVEL LOG

DATE:
STATE, COUNTRY:
WHERE I SLEPT:

WHO I WENT WITH:
FAVORITE MOMENT:

DATE:
STATE, COUNTRY:
WHERE I SLEPT:

WHO I WENT WITH:
FAVORITE MOMENT:

MY TRAVEL LOG

DATE:
STATE, COUNTRY:
WHERE I SLEPT:

WHO I WENT WITH:
FAVORITE MOMENT:

DATE:
STATE, COUNTRY:
WHERE I SLEPT:

WHO I WENT WITH:
FAVORITE MOMENT:

I WAS HERE

MY TRAVEL LOG

DATE:
STATE, COUNTRY:
WHERE I SLEPT:

WHO I WENT WITH:
FAVORITE MOMENT:

DATE:
STATE, COUNTRY:
WHERE I SLEPT:

WHO I WENT WITH:
FAVORITE MOMENT:

MY TRAVEL LOG

DATE:
STATE, COUNTRY:
WHERE I SLEPT:

WHO I WENT WITH:
FAVORITE MOMENT:

DATE:
STATE, COUNTRY:
WHERE I SLEPT:

WHO I WENT WITH:
FAVORITE MOMENT:

I WAS HERE

MY TRAVEL LOG

DATE:
STATE, COUNTRY:
WHERE I SLEPT:

WHO I WENT WITH:
FAVORITE MOMENT:

DATE:
STATE, COUNTRY:
WHERE I SLEPT:

WHO I WENT WITH:
FAVORITE MOMENT:

MY TRAVEL LOG

DATE:
STATE, COUNTRY:
WHERE I SLEPT:

WHO I WENT WITH:
FAVORITE MOMENT:

DATE:
STATE, COUNTRY:
WHERE I SLEPT:

WHO I WENT WITH:
FAVORITE MOMENT:

I WAS HERE

MY TRAVEL LOG

DATE:
STATE, COUNTRY:
WHERE I SLEPT:

WHO I WENT WITH:
FAVORITE MOMENT:

DATE:
STATE, COUNTRY:
WHERE I SLEPT:

WHO I WENT WITH:
FAVORITE MOMENT:

MY TRAVEL LOG

DATE:
STATE, COUNTRY:
WHERE I SLEPT:

WHO I WENT WITH:
FAVORITE MOMENT:

DATE:
STATE, COUNTRY:
WHERE I SLEPT:

WHO I WENT WITH:
FAVORITE MOMENT:

I WAS HERE

MY TRAVEL LOG

DATE:
STATE, COUNTRY:
WHERE I SLEPT:

WHO I WENT WITH:
FAVORITE MOMENT:

DATE:
STATE, COUNTRY:
WHERE I SLEPT:

WHO I WENT WITH:
FAVORITE MOMENT:

MY TRAVEL LOG

DATE:
STATE, COUNTRY:
WHERE I SLEPT:

WHO I WENT WITH:
FAVORITE MOMENT:

DATE:
STATE, COUNTRY:
WHERE I SLEPT:

WHO I WENT WITH:
FAVORITE MOMENT:

I WAS HERE

MY TRAVEL LOG

DATE:
STATE, COUNTRY:
WHERE I SLEPT:

WHO I WENT WITH:
FAVORITE MOMENT:

DATE:
STATE, COUNTRY:
WHERE I SLEPT:

WHO I WENT WITH:
FAVORITE MOMENT:

MY TRAVEL LOG

DATE:
STATE, COUNTRY:
WHERE I SLEPT:

WHO I WENT WITH:
FAVORITE MOMENT:

DATE:
STATE, COUNTRY:
WHERE I SLEPT:

WHO I WENT WITH:
FAVORITE MOMENT:

I WAS HERE

MY TRAVEL LOG

DATE:
STATE, COUNTRY:
WHERE I SLEPT:

WHO I WENT WITH:
FAVORITE MOMENT:

DATE:
STATE, COUNTRY:
WHERE I SLEPT:

WHO I WENT WITH:
FAVORITE MOMENT:

MY TRAVEL LOG

DATE:
STATE, COUNTRY:
WHERE I SLEPT:

WHO I WENT WITH:
FAVORITE MOMENT:

DATE:
STATE, COUNTRY:
WHERE I SLEPT:

WHO I WENT WITH:
FAVORITE MOMENT:

I WAS HERE

MY TRAVEL LOG

DATE:
STATE, COUNTRY:
WHERE I SLEPT:

WHO I WENT WITH:
FAVORITE MOMENT:

DATE:
STATE, COUNTRY:
WHERE I SLEPT:

WHO I WENT WITH:
FAVORITE MOMENT:

MY TRAVEL LOG

DATE:
STATE, COUNTRY:
WHERE I SLEPT:

WHO I WENT WITH:
FAVORITE MOMENT:

DATE:
STATE, COUNTRY:
WHERE I SLEPT:

WHO I WENT WITH:
FAVORITE MOMENT:

I WAS HERE

MY TRAVEL LOG

DATE:
STATE, COUNTRY:
WHERE I SLEPT:

WHO I WENT WITH:
FAVORITE MOMENT:

DATE:
STATE, COUNTRY:
WHERE I SLEPT:

WHO I WENT WITH:
FAVORITE MOMENT:

MY TRAVEL LOG

DATE:
STATE, COUNTRY:
WHERE I SLEPT:

WHO I WENT WITH:
FAVORITE MOMENT:

DATE:
STATE, COUNTRY:
WHERE I SLEPT:

WHO I WENT WITH:
FAVORITE MOMENT:

I WAS HERE

MY TRAVEL LOG

DATE:
STATE, COUNTRY:
WHERE I SLEPT:

WHO I WENT WITH:
FAVORITE MOMENT:

DATE:
STATE, COUNTRY:
WHERE I SLEPT:

WHO I WENT WITH:
FAVORITE MOMENT:

MY TRAVEL LOG

DATE:
STATE, COUNTRY:
WHERE I SLEPT:

WHO I WENT WITH:
FAVORITE MOMENT:

DATE:
STATE, COUNTRY:
WHERE I SLEPT:

WHO I WENT WITH:
FAVORITE MOMENT:

I WAS HERE

MY TRAVEL LOG

DATE:
STATE, COUNTRY:
WHERE I SLEPT:

WHO I WENT WITH:
FAVORITE MOMENT:

DATE:
STATE, COUNTRY:
WHERE I SLEPT:

WHO I WENT WITH:
FAVORITE MOMENT:

MY TRAVEL LOG

DATE:
STATE, COUNTRY:
WHERE I SLEPT:

WHO I WENT WITH:
FAVORITE MOMENT:

DATE:
STATE, COUNTRY:
WHERE I SLEPT:

WHO I WENT WITH:
FAVORITE MOMENT:

I WAS HERE

MY TRAVEL LOG

DATE:
STATE, COUNTRY:
WHERE I SLEPT:

WHO I WENT WITH:
FAVORITE MOMENT:

DATE:
STATE, COUNTRY:
WHERE I SLEPT:

WHO I WENT WITH:
FAVORITE MOMENT:

MY TRAVEL LOG

DATE:
STATE, COUNTRY:
WHERE I SLEPT:

WHO I WENT WITH:
FAVORITE MOMENT:

DATE:
STATE, COUNTRY:
WHERE I SLEPT:

WHO I WENT WITH:
FAVORITE MOMENT:

I WAS HERE

MY TRAVEL LOG

DATE:
STATE, COUNTRY:
WHERE I SLEPT:

WHO I WENT WITH:
FAVORITE MOMENT:

DATE:
STATE, COUNTRY:
WHERE I SLEPT:

WHO I WENT WITH:
FAVORITE MOMENT:

MY TRAVEL LOG

DATE:
STATE, COUNTRY:
WHERE I SLEPT:

WHO I WENT WITH:
FAVORITE MOMENT:

DATE:
STATE, COUNTRY:
WHERE I SLEPT:

WHO I WENT WITH:
FAVORITE MOMENT:

I WAS HERE

MY TRAVEL LOG

DATE:
STATE, COUNTRY:
WHERE I SLEPT:

WHO I WENT WITH:
FAVORITE MOMENT:

DATE:
STATE, COUNTRY:
WHERE I SLEPT:

WHO I WENT WITH:
FAVORITE MOMENT:

To live is the rarest thing of all.
 Most people exist, that is all.

Oscar Wilde

Live it up!

I WAS HERE

Other Books With Soul Journals:
Words I Want to Say
Every Breath- A Journal of Gratitude & Blessings
Crazy Ramblings of a Pregnant Woman
Remember When: Guest Book
Camp Memories
Reflections from the Beach
The Plan
The Adventures of US

Anniversary editions available on Amazon:
1st Anniversary: One Epic Year
5th Anniversary: Five Epic Years
10th Anniversary: Ten Epic Years
15th Anniversary: Fifteen Epic Years
20th Anniversary: Twenty Epic Years
25th Anniversary: Twenty-five Epic Years
30th Anniversary: Thirty Epic Years
35th Anniversary: Thirty-five Epic Years
40th Anniversary: Forty Epic Years
45th Anniversary: Forty-five Epic Years
50th Anniversary: Fifty Epic Years

Perfect Anniversary Gift

Books With Soul

Books with Soul believes in sharing gifts that inspire and motivate others to create memories and keep a record of the story of their life.
What if... you had a record of your memories or someone you loved?

INSPIRATION COMES IN ALL SIZES, SHAPES AND IDEAS

WE believe every life is worth a few written words to pass on or reflect on in the future.
You don't have to be an author to tell the story of your life. Just be you.
Today will someday be the good old days, remember them.
Books with Soul offers inspirational journals with questions & thoughts
to help record memories for the most novice of journalers. Birthday, milestones, wedding and baby gifts. Help someone write their life story.

Questions? Email info@bookswithsoul.com
We appreciate every reader, every traveler and recorder of history.
We would love if you took the time to write a
review on Amazon and let us know if the books motivated you.

Find more journals, inspiration, diaries, coloring books and gifts for every milestone at:
www.bookswithsoul.com

If you would like to have a personalized journal for
an organization, company, group, club, or activity, contact Books with Soul.
Special unique journals in 25 quantities or more can be created.

*if someone bought you this journal, pay it forward and
buy a journal
for someone you care about.
Help them write the story of their life.

I WAS HERE

Books with Soul ™

was inspired from a lover of music and life, who believed in the soul.

He had a collection of wonderful things. Physical memories you could

read, touch, and listen to- including thousands of vinyl albums.

Old school music, that lasts forever. In 2018, he passed away from brain cancer, but his memory lives on as others go old school. Collect pieces

of your history, put pencil to paper, and record written memories.

A physical book will not be lost in the cloud, and will last longer than a lifetime.

Keep a record of the story of your life. Your Words. Your Pages.

This is for you Mark.

Thanks for taking the time to write a year of memories.

Keep this journal somewhere safe.

START A YEARLY COLLECTION.

OR

GIFT ONE AS A SPECIAL GIFT

A VARIETY OF JOURNALS EXIST: TRY ONE WITH DAILY INSPIRATIONAL QUOTES, OR WRITING PROMPTS TO KEEP YOU WRITING.

GO TO THE WEBSITE FOR SALES & SWAG

Bookswithsoul.com
Your Words. Your Pages.

I WAS HERE

GET YOUR COPY OF INSIDER SECRETS

Check out Travel Secrets: Insider guide to planning, affording and taking more vacations on Amazon. Free on Kindle Unlimited.

Collect your memories.

I WAS HERE

Who knows what will Happen to our data in the future?

Celebrate the art of writing. Your words on paper to last a lifetime.

Check out *Books With Soul* Your Words. Your Pages.